Tristis Crisis: a collection of Emotion-Based pieces

Gabriel Schlegel

BookLeaf Publishing

India | USA | UK

Presentation by *BookLeaf Publishing*

Web: www.bookleafpub.com

E-mail: info@bookleafpub.com

ISBN: 9789357445948

First edition 2022

Soulmate

Soulmate.
What is that?
Those exist?
Where can I find one?

Are they hidden beneath my bed,
where I can't even see them?
Are they the ones I keep mistaking
as monsters in my head?

Or are they hidden in my closet,
where I can barely keep my
clothes and suits in order?
Could that probably be it?

Or are they instead hiding in plain sight,
zooming past the city I live in
or in the workplace I find myself in?
Hiding in the dead of night?

Or are they even in my home,
or are they even at my school?
Do they even exist?
How will I know when I've found my own
soulmate?

Truth be told, I thought I found my soulmate
within you. I felt a stirring in my heart,
a connection longing to be made.
And I thought I felt that within you, too,
but I suppose not.
It must have sadly been a ruse.

Can you help me find my soulmate,
if it is indeed not you?
That is, if they do exist --
if I must contemplate...

Could you maybe be
my soulmate, please?
I know I'd rather not wait
for what would be an eternity.

The Jubilee Line

When I got off the train, there was nobody there.
Not even you.
I looked around the empty space,
the oddly polished walls,
the strangely waxed floors-
I thought someone had been there.
My heart had hoped it was you,
But when I looked around, there was nothing
there.

I thought, after I had called out to you-
that late night, when I told you
I was going home and when we stayed on
the phone whilst I was riding through the
Jubilee line, riding late until the sun was rising-
I thought you'd be there. Though I
guess an absent part of me must have
expected such a thing, because when
I saw you weren't there, I smiled.
I grinned.
I laughed.
Jumped off the tracks and let out a huge
scream - "I'm back!"

Though, walking home, ascending from the

deepest caverns of that station, expecting
to see the warm sun welcome me and,
out into the lifeless streets,
I started to feel sad.
My neighborhood didn't feel like my own.
And though I know you'll see
the pain in my eyes,
and hear the obvious strain in my voice,
I still want you to be happy,
I still want to be there for you,
I want to keep my distance,
I want to be close.

Was that phone call for nothing?
Did the words you tell me that night,
that shared feeling we had,
mean nothing?
Or did your emotions get the better of you?
I've no idea, only you can say.
Though I'd like to believe that I'm wrong-
that those words and feelings we shared,
if even for a brief moment, did mean something.

I know you'll read this letter I wrote to you
soon enough. You're bound to come through
this station as well sooner or later.
I just hope you aren't alone when you do,
but if it is,
then you can catch me around the corner

and down two blocks, where I'll be holding
on to a small box that I've been waiting
to give you for a while.
But while you're on that train,
I'll always answer your calls,
all you need to do is put my number
in your phone and hit "Call."

A Whimper

I'm scared.
I'm so scared.

Scared of so many things.

Scared to lose the friendships
that I have now.

Scared that I'll never get a chance
to retry.

Scared of where I'm going to go.
Scared of where I've been.
Scared of where I could go.

All I want is for a soft guiding hand
to comfort me,
to tell me that it'll all be okay.

I'm scared of opening up again.
Scared of leaving my heart out there,
open and vulnerable.

My heart still has the tread marks

from everyone stampeding all over it,
walking and stepping all over it,
leaving their dusty imprints all over it.

I don't want to be scared anymore.
All I want to be is calm.
All I want to do is feel safe.
All I want to hear is that I'll be alright.

I'm scared.
I'm so scared.

Blackhole Void

A pulsing blackhole resides
where my heart once laid.
Walking past you is like
a singularity breaking out
into plurality – thoughts,
emotions, here it all comes,
whirling around,
sucking in and away at the sanity
and the broken crumbled walls
that I keep trying to build up.

A whirlwind of emotions
that were once balanced,
the memories that I was doing
so well at hiding away...
They're all worth nothing when
I hear your voice or see you walk
in the hallway.

My breath, I'm sure you've noticed,
it gets weird every time I walk past
you.

You've long forgotten,
probably still don't care,

but I can swear from time to time
I've seen you glance my way,
a momentary glance in my direction.
I can't tell if it's on accident.
Probably is.
You probably don't care.
You probably want me out of your mind
once and for all.
You said it yourself,
you can't ever see me
in the same way again.

But I'd still like to try.
I'd like to fill this black hole
that's been pulling at me
with what it was filled with before.
Positivity.
Light.

No

I don't want you to know I'm hurt.
I don't want you to know I'm in pain.
I don't want to hurt you.
I don't want to share this pain.
You have enough of your own.

Yes, I am holding my own emotions in.
Yes, I know I'm failing,
But if me trying keeps your happiness going,
I am fully willing to do so.

Yes, maybe I will open up if you nudge me,
if you just ask what's wrong.
Even if you won't be alright with the answer,
I still owe it to you to be open and honest.
You'd like that, wouldn't you?

I wasn't lying when I said I'm genuinely happy
for you.
I just wasn't honest when I said I wasn't hurt.

Your Melichrisis

You love so much and yet you
beat yourself up so much.
You love so hard, but so quickly you knock
yourself down.
With every move you make,
A new threat is born.
This is… something YOU'VE said.

Do you not see that the pain you're toiling
around with in your hands, do you not see
what it is made of?
It's made of your own self-doubt,
Of your own inability to realize that
you, too-
        Yes, you, forehead!-
deserve your own happiness.
You can find someone who you'll
find worthy, and no matter who that
may be, I would only like to ask
that I be there to support you,
no matter what.

They say I'm still blaming myself
that I'm not letting myself move on.
But the truth is, I found my own self forgiveness

a long time ago.
You may feel as though there is no reason to be
happy,
You may have abandoned your mantra-
you know the one, the one where it goes,
"In order to make others happy, you must be
happy yourself,"
The one that I'll always associate you by-
But I have not abandoned it.
I don't think I ever will.

I'll write my stories,
I'll scribble my poems,
But I'm tired of writing these
indirect letters. Of leaving
to chance whether or not you
see what I write to you.

So this is why I'm giving you this
directly. It is a great risk,
but it is a risk I need to take.

We all need to take risks.
You may regret what may happen if you
take the risk, but you'll hold an
even deeper regret, knowing you
didn't try, and one day you'll wish
you had taken that leap
of faith.

Because of you, I was asked a question:
"Why do you keep trying?"
I was genuinely confused.
I shrugged, not wanting to give them
the answer they already knew.

Butterfly Effect

When my mind has a thought,
it rushes through my entire body.
Something's causing it to tick
in an outrageously uplifting tone,
and like the lights coming on when someone
comes home late at night,
all begins to shine.

All at once, in a frantic fury,
I'm driven to action.
Worlds begin to crystalize
right before my very eyes.
Words describe things I never
once thought of before,
while sketched lines flesh out
the images that flash in
and out of my mind.

Time does not exist in this state.
Unlike other ideas,
time is one that gets graciously
ignored.
Sparks begin to fly about and
catch ablaze as my creations begin
to weave a mind of their own.

There is nothing that can slow it
down, except for its own conclusion.

These are the only chains that would
be welcomed by anybody and everybody.
They give off energy and inspiration
to whoever is nearby.
And as the consumer of this piece,
as the audience to this show,
we invite you to let this contagious
energy flow through you, so that
it may continue to spread
in other aspiring minds out there.

If-When

When I tell you
my heart can easily flutter,
do not, for even an instant,
doubt me.

If I say that
it does not take much to
brighten my day,
believe me.

I've got a childlike wonder
in my eyes
and a dream to conquer the world,
one pillowfort at a time.

If you hear I am one to jump
at the slightest hint of
opportunity,
take their word for it.

If I wish to travel the world
for all it has to offer,
come and join me,
I want to take you.

And if,
when in our silent moment of intimacy,
I tell you I love you,
I promise you,
I mean it with all my heart.

Tick Tock

Tick tock,
broken clock on the wall.
You're only right twice
in one day.

What will it take
to make you tick?
Do you just need a voice
So that you can tock?

How much time can I possibly have
When everything is melting away?
Everything and everybody, they all
keep changing on a whim and I
can't keep up!

How can I possibly leave my mark on
the sands of time if the sands keep
moving away from me? How can I
grasp my shot if I don't have the
motivation to reach out for it?

Turbulent times, and that
bloody clock keeps on ticking.
First it was broken, now it's working?

I regret giving it a voice so that it it
could tock, because now it'll just keep
on going and going and here I am,
along for the ride. The hands
and handles are all mishandling
me and I just can't handle this.

So, how much time can I truly have?
And what if I run out of time?
Where do I go then? What do I do?
What do I say?

Tick tock,
once-broken clock on the wall.
I regret granting you a voice,
because now you're wasting it all.

Wasting it on things
I could care less about,
brushing away too quickly what
I care too much for.

And that pessimistic ticking
of yours is ticking me off.

If only I could will myself to
rob you of that annoying
voice of yours.
Yet it'd be all too cruel of me
to just simply remove your batteries.

Tick, tock.
Tick, tock.
I keep hearing it throughout
the halls. Mother Time, you're
either my enemy or my friend.
Which is it?

Tick tock,
working clock in my head,
you can rest your voice for tomorrow.
It's time for bed.
And I will choose to ignore you instead.

Empath

Isn't it funny how so interconnected
we all can be?
When we put aside the pettiness,
the grittiness,
the overall toils of life,
we're really not so different,
you and I.

We're all connected through
our hearts.
We bleed,
we sing,
we're born,
we die,
we live again,
we bleed again.
We love,
we lie,
we fight,
we make up,
we make out,
we cave in,
we give up,
we fall,
we rise,

we die,
we're revived again!

Our heart beats in unison,
even though they never started that way.
And it's a truth that's as evident as
the reality of night and day.

So why do you
treat them different,
see them different,
speak to them different,
breathe around them different,
bereave them for a different
reason, because they are different
from what you see as normal and not different?

Do we not treat each other the same?
Trust each other the same?
Cheat on each other the same
and lie with one another just the same?
Do we not question ourselves just the same,
doubt ourselves just the same,
give up on the game all just the same
as we look for anyone other than ourselves to
blame
for the rising shame in neglect that's become the
bane
of our existence, all of that just the same?

For shame.
It seems our stubbornness, our disdain,
our inability to share each other's pain,
has flushed our dreams out the river
and backed it down the drain.

Years

Days
turn to weeks
turn to months
turn to years.

Where I stood
once shallow,
I've taken back
my tears.

Emotions,
once rampant,
today not so
severe,

my only wish,
platonic,
is that you
were still here.

The sky,
it flickers,
your memories
are near,

Memories --
they play on --
of you there
and me here.

Though you
can only watch
as I
persevere,

I wish,
platonic,
that you were
still here.

Gone,
you're not,
but still,
ever clear,

your presence,
once stood,
it's impact,
so sheer.

Days
turn to weeks
turn to months
turn to years.

I wish
you are proud
of today's lack
of tears.

Your voice,
unheard
for a few more
years,

it excites me,
amuses me,
to stick to rules,
adhered.

And so be it be,
that I stand
with a future
unclear,

I wish
one day,
platonic,
to see you here

Days
turn to weeks

turn to months
turn to years.

And through
the passing of days
and the drying
of tears,

You and I
shall stand,
platonic,
together here.

Your laughter,
your words,
I'll clearly
hear,

but only with
the quick passing
of just a few more
years.

Self-cast Doubt

In the light of dawn,
there is inspiration.
There is so much to create.
So much to see.
So much to overshadow with
our own greatness.
At times, we may feel as though
we are not actually worthy of
this light.
But yet, that may just be
simple doubt, a blindness
cast upon us only because of
our over-familiarity with what
we create.
We may grow to despise our art,
to want to scrap it and move on
to the next grand project.
But remember, not everyone has
seen the process. Not everyone has
experienced its birth the way you have.
Think of it like a child, in that sense.
It's something new for people to meet,
to see, to experience.
At times, we are our own harshest critic,

serving only to cast down our greatness
to the greater depths of obscurity.
But before sending it away,
let another refreshing set of eyes
see what you have so far.
Embrace the roughness
and accept the criticism.
It just might breathe new life
and confidence into your
weary artist soul.

Hope

A peculiar thing, hope is.
How it guides us,
how it gives us a reason to be
stubborn as ever.

The heart wants what
the heart wants.
Even when the mind knows
it's impossible,
even when the soul knows
its improbable,
the hear will always want
what it wants.

With this blinding substance
called "Hope,"
I hope to be able to control it
and channel it into something
that can possibly help.
Something that can give back
what it's taking,
what it's holding.

I hope to have so much hope,
that my heart can't handle

the excess,
and the only way I'll be able to
get rid of it is by giving it away
to someone who needs hope
just a little more than I do.

Backcover

sometimes the heart wants
what the heart wants
because it doesn't know what else
to want.
why would you keep looking
for something when you
think it's standing right there
in front of you?
you become blind to the
possibilities and end up
blindsighting yourself,
making yourself so
close-minded to the possibilities
that await you beyond your
rose-tinted glasses and
insatiable desire for the thing
you can't have.
the pain is poetic in and of itself,
and it is through the art of pain
that i, your humble writer,
offer my metaphysical hand
to you, the humble reader,
to guide you through the indesirable,
to paint you and cover you in the
light of reality,

and to finally let you open your eyes,
see the light,
to the things that want you
more than you wanting the
thing you so desperately want
but cannot have.

Blissdream

In this field of flowers,
past the den with the sleeping cubs
and stalking young lions,
there's a part of me that wishes to be here,
to stay ignorant forever.

It's so peaceful here, and I would give
anything to stay here.
You can feel the dew just drip off the nearby
grass blades, landing on your bare foot as
they brush by.

You can do anything. You can run, you can
walk,
you can frolic around if you so wish. The world
here is your stage, and you can act however
you want. Nothing but the curious cub
and the tired lion will watch you anyhow,
to see what you do, and how you do it.

The sun is at a perfect angle,
the sky is a perfect orange and yellow blend.
The air is nice and calm, like a mild day in
spring.

What I wouldn't give to soak up this world,
to relish in all of the beauty that it has, and
instead of trampling it's beauty, to share it
with everyone else who needs it.

Running on E

The feeling is there,
the motivation isn't.
Something's keeping me going,
keeping me inspired somehow,
though I'm not sure what.
Could it be the fact I'm close
to the finish line?
Or is it the sleep deprivation taking over?
Is it the lack of care of whatever
I put down,
or--
is it careful thinking and planning
seeing me through to the end?

I probably shouldn't question it,
It's never really wise to
look a gift horse in the mouth.
Something's keeping me going,
and though I'm not sure what,
I may as well keep going with
the flow.

I'm sure once I'm a bit more
aware of myself, I'll
figure out what it is keeping me going.

...what if it's procrastination keeping me going?

Tick Tock: Shattered Clock

Tick tock,
shattered clock from the wall.
'Twas only a matter of time
before you decided to fall.

Nobody can blame you.
Many despised you,
doing as you were created to do.
Many wanted to strip you of
your voice,
forever desolate.

You moved in a different direction
from us. Pushing yourself against
the grain, moving, in our eyes,
way too fast to keep up.

Did you decide to fall?
Or did somebody force you?

I'm hard-pressed to admit,
at one point I was not your friend.

I lamented, wrote bad words
about you, hushing you.
But I have grown since that time.

Where I once chose to ignore you,
and all of your calls, I see now
that was my mistake, my downfall -
for ignoring you was the thing that
set you off, made you move as
fast as you did,
so DESPERATE for an answer.

Love and heartbreak,
sunshine and tornadoes.
Happening in the blink of an eye.
Happening as you kept ticking,
kept tocking your way through
life, as you were created to do.

Perhaps I was wrong to try
to fight that which is uncontrollable.
Perhaps, in my own lament,
in my own remains of my heart,
laying listless on the floor,
it is I who caused time to go by
so fast.

Was it me, in the end,
who silenced your voice?

Everything's a blur.
Can't even tell you for sure what
I did yesterday or the day before
at this point.

Tick, tock.
Tick, tock.
Your voice haunts my mind,
the images I have of you
in my brain recede into
a shoreline of regret and misery,
the sands made coarse by the years
of experience of a life that I am still living.

And now here I am, a mess.
Shattered as you are on the floor right now,
I keep hearing your voice.
I keep hearing your tick.
I keep hearing your tock.

In your final cries, in your
receding repetitive little noises,
a different memory plays.
A slideshow going on in my mind,
reminding me of what was, what currently is,
and what could have been.

Though I lament, I admit
I was too harsh, so long ago.

I now crave for similar times,
the ones when I would talk
so poorly about you,
the times when I begged you
to shut up.

The world's crazy now.
There's so much confusion.
I can't make sense of anything.

Heart's been shattered,
true colors have been revealed,
self-reflection is everywhere,
not just in the mirror or in the
ponds that you left behind.

And it all plays on a loop,
as I hear you tick,
as I hear you tock.

Tick tock,
once-solid clock.
A noise I once desperately
tried to block.

It's a noise I want back.
In the chambers of my mind
I still hear your ticking,
echoing,

echoing,
until the reverb turns it
into cognitive dissonance.

How I once hated it,
how I would count off every
half-second before your next
tock ticked off.

But perhaps, instead of sitting
here, lamenting about what could
have been and what was...
Perhaps I should perceive this
tragedy in a softer, more welcoming light.

There are many other clocks
on the walls of department stores
and cleaned-up school buildings.
They still tick on all the same,
and these days, not even a
simple shortage of power
can stop them from telling off the
correct time.

Though we may grieve for
clocks which have met a fate
similar to yours,
we too must keep ticking off
seconds,

minutes,
hours,
eventual days,
eventual weeks.

Time waits for no man, woman,
or child. And just as Father Time
keeps his own sands of time flowing,
we too must be open to carry on.
To forgive, yet not to forget.
To yearn, yet not to let it envelop our
true selves.

Tick, tock.
Tick, tock.
I embrace your death and
the shards you left.

Though I'll miss how I
despised your ticking
and your tocking,
I will not let it hold me back
from pursuing my own worth
in time.
Tick tock,
shattered clock,
you've done all that you could.
And standing strong now,
I can do all that I once said I would.

And like many of my friends have said,
This is something that indeed I should.

Strain

When we had to be forced apart,
when we all felt the strain,
there were these thoughts
that wouldn't cease –
they would simply remain.

We've grown distant.
I don't mean physically, I think
that's pretty obvious at this point.

But I mean distant as in
actually talking.
We hardly get to properly talk
these days.

Ever since that one day,
you've seemed tense.
And I keep worrying it's
something I did, or if it's
just stress from everything
going on.

I don't know what to do,
and it's driving me crazy,
more so than having to be

apart from you.

What am I supposed to do?
I'm trying to keep my own
sanity, that would make things
worse, if things aren't already
as bad as they can be.

I want to apologize a million
times over but even that would
cause a bit more tension between
us, wouldn't it?

There's too many uncertainties.
What am I supposed to do?
I want to help,
I want to be able to comfort you,
to make you feel better,
like I always did before everything
happened between us.

Was it really me?
No, I can't ask that either.
There's too many things
I want to ask that I just can't.
I don't want to make things worse.

I want to give you time to
recover, but I also don't

want to feel like I did something
to make you so cold towards me.

Can't I just ask for clarity?
Can't I just ask for all of that?
Or am I just going to have
to wait until this all blows
over to get everything in order?

I'm worried about you,
I care about you.
I don't want to annoy you.
But what if I already have?

I'm worried about you,
I care about you.
I don't want to annoy you.
But what if I already have?

It's a question I keep asking myself,
over and over,
like a record on repeat, complete
with the stuttering and the annoyance
and the desire for it to continue on
to something else, something new.

If it's me, tell me, please.
I can't keep going this crazy over
these scenarios that I keep playing

in my mind on repeat.

I can't, I can't, I can't.

Once we all get back together,
I need to set things right with you.
I need to apologize for what I did
before everything went down,
and how I acted in the earlier days
of this lockdown.

I need something here,
either a sense of closure
or forgiveness and a place
to continue.

If it's something I did,
if it's something I'm doing,
then I'm sorry. Really, truly.

If it isn't anything I did, then
I'm still sorry for how I'm acting now.

The stress, when we were put in global
quarantine,
has put us under an unspeakable strain,
one where we can't bare to talk to
each other for one reason or another.

Things were just starting to look
up for us, weren't they?
And things will continue to look
up for us once this is all over.

However we reach that outcome though
is something we'll need to figure out
when the time comes.

We can't keep doing this,
in all honesty. I'm pretty sure
this is my fault, really,
my fault for overthinking.
And if it is, I'm sorry.

My mind keeps going back to
the last day we were together,
when you seemed so tense,
when I wanted to try to cheer
you up but you shoo'd me away.
One of those rare times where
my presence wouldn't be the solution,
but instead started to become the problem.

You were so tense, and things sort of
spiraled down as the days went on.
All I want to do is try to cheer you
up like I used to. I'm blinding myself.
Curse my stubbornness!

As the days go on, the pandemic seems
to be flattening out. And even though
things are starting to look up between
the both of us again, a part of me
still thinks that it could be, at the very most,
a facade. There's still something there,
something slightly tense, and until we
get things back on track, it'll be as if
I'm walking in a landmine blindfolded.
Even still I hope that I'm wrong with
my thoughts, like I usually am when
I overthink something to this extent.

We've got a lot of catching up to do,
you and I. And I hope that seeing
each other in person will help set things
back on track, the way they were before
everything hit us the way it did.

I've got your back, no matter what.
I promised you that before
when we were first starting to be
friends, and I'm just reminding
you now that no matter what,
I've got your back.

We've fallen out of touch,
yeah maybe that's my fault.

Whoops-
You can forgive me though, right?

I've been a bit busy with my own stuff,
school's getting on my nerves a bit,
everything's due next week
and I haven't really been able to
breathe.

How've you been though?
Keeping afloat?
Anything going on?
...yeah this is kind of awkward,
I'm making it kind of awkward now,
aren't I? Heh-

Even though we haven't been as close
as we have been in the past,
just know I haven't forgotten about you.
I'm not trying to ditch you.
I mean, I've already tried and failed
before. We're already stuck
with each other, no changing that, haha.

Don't be afraid to text me ever,
aright? I could use a distraction from everything,
and I'm awful at pulling myself
away from my stuff.

Once we can come back together,
don't worry – we should
definitely be able to talk
more like we used to.

We're still friends 'til the end, right?
Right!
Alright then, it's settled!

After this is over, we're definitely hanging
out. More than those five minute
visits I keep doing. We've got
some stuff to catch up on!
I want to see you smile again.
I promise you I'll cheer you
up the same way I always did
before, maybe this time
even better than before!

*But in hindsight, I could never be the one
to pick you up from the ground.
I thought this was a battle to be won,
but look where I'm at now...*

Tristis Crisis

I still can't believe I cried over you last night.
I never thought it possible
to have loved someone as much as I have loved
you.

I imagined a conversation with you last night,
actually.
And that's what broke me.
I wish you could have found me somewhat
appealing.
I wish I was worthy of a second chance.
I tried everything I could and yet, it didn't work
out.
And I'll never truly understand why it couldn't.

I wanted to give you the whole world,
because to be honest, my love?
You were my whole world.
You were the sun that lit me up on my cloudiest
days.
You were the spark that kept my fire going.

And I hoped, for every day that I tried so hard
for one more chance with you, that I was making
you feel the same way.

When I cried,
I didn't feel relief.
I instead felt dread.
Dread for what I didn't do
And what I wished I did.
Sadness, because the plan I had
Come up with would never come to
fruition.
Hurt and dejected, because all of the effort
I put in for us ended up being for nothing.

I felt sorry for not being the one for you.
And though I wanted to appear happy for you,
you could see right through my facade.

Perhaps the sun is blinding,
and perhaps the smoke from the fires is
as visceral as they may seem to be from
afar, but this didn't matter to me.
None of it did.

My heart wanted you,
and the heart will always want
what it wants.
Even if the brain knows it to be
an improbability.
Love knows no bounds.

I still can't believe I cried over you last night.
I never thought it possible
to have loved someone as much as I have loved
you.
I never thought that it wouldn't be possible
to get that kind of love returned,
as desperately as I wanted it to be.

Vale, vetus amicus

In my mind are memories,
of just the two of us.
And with them comes a foreign phrase,
"Vale, vetus amicus."

Our laughter swells as time, it flees,
yet all good things must end.
It pains a lot for me to say.
"Goodbye, my dear old friend."

Your voice echoes for eternity,
your image fades to dust.
Yet here I am with a strong facade, saying
"Vale, vetus amicus."

From heated arguments to blissful glee,
to letting that last message send.
How fitting is it we parted with,
"Goodbye, my dear old friend."

But there's still life, lest you not believe,
and time to reconcile.
Though we may be far apart, you'll see
we'll still be friends for quite a while.

My mind remembers the two of us,
and I'm sad it had to end.
Vale, vetus amicus.
Goodbye, my dear old friend.

Stranger

Perhaps it was never meant to be.
Perhaps there is such a thing as
The right one in the wrong place.
Perhaps it really does make all
the difference in the world.

Perhaps,
in another timeline,
it WAS meant to be.
That's an optimistic thought,
now isn't it?
But we don't live in that timeline.

The station's gone cold, you know.
It's.... there's nothing here.
The next train out of here doesn't come
for another few hours and all I've got
is this pen a few pieces of paper.
And my thoughts,
but you never want to leave someone alone in a
cold,
abandoned place with their thoughts.

If there was ever enough time,
I'd probably get to know you more.

I'd get to see what makes you tick,
what makes your brain work.
I could at least get to know your name,
who you are,
what you like and
what you don't like.

But perhaps,
Just maybe perhaps,
there's better things to do than to sit around,
wallowing in despair for someone
I apparently didn't even know.

Perhaps it was never meant to be.
Perhaps there is such a thing as
The right one in the wrong place.
Perhaps it really does make all
the difference in the world.

The train's pulling up to the station.
Is it that timc, already?
Time to move on.

9 789357 445948